WHAT YOUR
FISH NEEDS

—— By Mike Wickham ——

A Dorling Kindersley Book

Dorsal fin
Lateral line
Eye
Nostril
Scales
Caudal fin
Mouth
Gill cover
Anal fin
Anal fin
Pectoral fin

WHAT YOUR FISH NEEDS

	Less	1	2	3	4	5	More
Time commitment		✓					
Exercise		✓					
Play time		✓					
Space requirements		✓					
Grooming		✓					
Feeding			✓				
Cleaning up				✓			
Life span		✓					
Good with kids 5 to 10				✓			
Good with kids 10 and over						✓	

CONTENTS

FOREWORD BY BRUCE FOGLE, DVM

Around twenty-five years ago, a psychiatrist at the University of Pennsylvania, Dr. Aaron Katcher, carried out a curious little experiment. He took people's blood pressure under a variety of different circumstances. You have probably already guessed that when he observed people looking at a fish tank filled with plants and tropical fish, their blood pressure drops. He noted that people suffering from high blood

Green sailfin molly

pressure had an even greater than average drop, and when stressed by a test after watching the fish tank, people's blood pressure still rose, but not as high as it had been before watching the fish. Watching fish, he concluded, is good for you, medically speaking.

Curious isn't it? Just watching attractive little fish glide around in a well-maintained tank is physically beneficial. Dentists have known this for years, which is why so many have fish tanks at their clinics. Dr. Katcher was, in fact, the faculty psychiatrist at the University of Pennsylvania's Dental School. (When I asked him why a dental school employed a psychiatrist, he grinned, Cheshire-like, and replied, "Pain.") His interest in our relationship with the animal world attracted him to the university's Veterinary School, which is where he carried out most of his studies.

One of the things Dr. Katcher said is that we evolved as beings who were part of the natural world, but,now that we have separated ourselves from so much of it we instinctively "bring the outdoors indoors" by surrounding ourselves with nature in the form of plants or tanks of tropical fish.

Black balloon molly

There are other reasons for contemplating having a fish tank in your home or office. Aside from the physiological benefits, a tank is just plain beautiful. The variety of colors and shapes of freshwater tropical fish is marvellous; their behavior is fascinating.

But if you plan to set up a tank, there are obligations. They may be fish, far removed from you in their watery world, but they are still living creatures. It is up to you to make sure you are creating an ideal environment for them. That includes knowing not only about their needs, but also about their behavior. Some species, pretty as they are, are predators to others.

Getting off to the right start with your fish is the best preventive medicine I can suggest. This little book helps set you on the right course toward what I hope will be a fruitful and mutually rewarding relationship.

While it's true that you can't hold your fish in your lap or cuddle it while you watch television, fish have personalities. As you watch them, you'll get to know your fish as individuals.

DOMESTICATING FISH

Exploring off the Gulf Coast in Florida.

Fish have been with us for a very long time – 500 million years! They are the very first vertebrates (animals with backbones). However, the first fish were a bit different from the animals we think of as fish today. They had gills but no fins or jaws. Their backbones were made of cartilage. One could say that the first fish looked more like tadpoles covered with plates than fish. It would be around another 100 million years before fins, jaws, and true bony skeletons developed.

Four hundred million years later, we have the staggering diversity of fish that are found in oceans, lakes, river, streams, ponds, and puddles all over the globe today. All the various species of fish we now keep in aquariums were originally collected wild from rivers, streams, and lakes throughout the world.

Most aquarium species are tropical. That is, they come from warm regions of the world, especially from South America and southeast Asia, and we typically decorate our aquariums with aquatic plants to mimic the habitat along the edge of tropical streams in those areas.

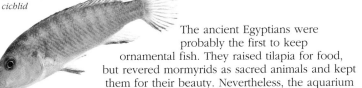

Cobalt blue cichlid

The ancient Egyptians were probably the first to keep ornamental fish. They raised tilapia for food, but revered mormyrids as sacred animals and kept them for their beauty. Nevertheless, the aquarium fish with the best documented domestication history is from a more temperate climate. Yes, I'm speaking of the goldfish.

Modern aquarium-keeping, using glass aquariums, developed in the mid 1800s. Those early aquariums had no pumps, filters, heaters, or light units. This equipment – which really is vital to your fish's well-being – did not become common until the 1950s.

The hobby as we know it today took shape around the 1930s. In those days, wild fish were captured and shipped by boat in metal cans. The long voyages meant high losses, but the availability of shiny new species whetted the public's appetite for fishkeeping. Today, commercial airlines handle the shipping of fish. The fish are packed in plastic bags inflated with pure oxygen for a journey that is much shorter and safer. And these days, most aquarium fish are not caught in the wild. They're captive raised on commercial fish farms, making the journey from source to your aquarium even shorter.

Golden barb

Japanese moor, a species of fancy goldfish. Over 1,000 years ago, the Chinese developed goldfish by selectively breeding a variety of carp. Today, there are dozens of varieties of this single species – all selectively bred by humans.

CHOOSING YOUR AQUARIUM

An aquarium is a house for fish. To properly house your fish, you need:
• A strong stand (the foundation)
• A tank (the house itself)
• A cover with light (the roof)

Before you choose your aquarium, decide where you want to put it. Pick a location that is not too near a window, because excess sunlight can cause algae problems. Pick a safe spot. For example, an aquarium placed near a door may be smashed when the wind blows the door open and it slams against the tank. Be sure there is an electrical outlet nearby to provide power for all your equipment. Consider how much space is available and measure it to be sure you know exactly how much room you have.

THE STAND

Aquariums weigh approximately ten pounds per gallon when they're filled. Your aquarium stand must be strong enough to hold all this weight and sturdy enough not to wobble. Stands that wobble can cause your aquarium to twist and break. While you may have furniture that is strong enough to hold an aquarium safely, it is usually best to buy a commercial aquarium stand.

Choose a size that fits the footprint (length and width on the bottom) of the tank you plan to buy. Wrought-iron stands are inexpensive choices that usually leave you space to place a second aquarium on the shelf beneath. Cabinet stands are much better, though. There is plenty of room inside the cabinet to store food, fish nets, and other supplies. Plus, the cabinet does a much better job of hiding electrical cords and air lines.

THE TANK

Aquarium tanks come in sizes from a single gallon up to a monstrous 300 gallons. The 10-, 20-, 29-, 55-, 75-, and 135-gallon models offer the best buys. Always choose the largest size you can afford. Larger

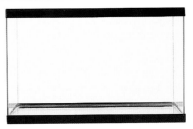

aquariums provide a more stable environment and, believe it or not, take approximately the same time to maintain. Yes, bigger is better, but a bigger footprint is better yet! The footprint of your aquarium determines how much water surface there will be for absorbing oxygen, and how much bottom area there will be for fish to claim as territory. So, a typical 20-gallon long aquarium (30-x-12-inch footprint) is a better choice than a 20-gallon high aquarium (24-x-12-inch footprint), even though both hold 20 gallons.

Glass aquariums are most common – and most economical – but many hobbyists prefer acrylic aquariums because they are stronger, lighter, more transparent, and have rounded corners. Acrylic aquariums scratch more easily, though. Rectangular aquariums are most popular, but pentagons, hexagons, and octagons are also available. Exotic bubble, clock tower, and coffee table shaped aquariums are difficult to maintain and should be avoided.

THE LIGHT

Lighting systems help you see your fish. Most also cover the tank to reduce evaporation and keep the fish from jumping out. Plants need light, too. If you plan to keep live plants, choose a lighting system that provides two to five watts of light per gallon.

A full hood with fluorescent light.

A full-hood with fluorescent bulb often offers the easiest lighting solution for viewing fish. However, it provides a low level of light that is suitable for only the hardiest aquatic plants. Full-hoods are fine with plastic plants. A glass canopy and strip light combination is more versatile, because you can add in additional strip lights to keep your aquatic plants happy.

Power compact fluorescent lighting systems use U-shaped bulbs that offer even more punch for lighting the planted aquarium. Metal halide pendent lights hang above the aquarium and provide intense light, but they can be very expensive.

FILTRATION FOR FISH

In the wild, there may be hundreds, thousands, or even millions of gallons of water per fish. Compared to nature, aquariums are crowded. Filters enable us to keep more fish in a smaller space.

YOUR FILTER SYSTEM MUST PERFORM THREE FUNCTIONS

• **Mechanical filtration:** The physical straining of solid waste particles from the water. Filter pads or similar media collect fish feces, uneaten food, and debris. Most filters provide mechanical filtration.

• **Biological filtration:** A natural process, whereby helpful bacteria become established in the aquarium and convert harmful wastes to harmless substances. All filters provide some degree of biological filtration. Some are much better than others, though. Of the three types of filtration, biological is probably the most important.

• **Chemical filtration:** Uses adsorptive compounds to remove dissolved wastes from the aquarium. Activated carbon is the most well-known chemical filter medium. These products adsorb finite amounts of waste and must be replaced regularly.

STYLES OF FILTERS

Outside power filters are the most popular choice today. They are priced reasonably and are easy to use. An outside power filter hangs on the back of your aquarium. The built-in motor pulls water from the aquarium and pumps it through filtering media inside the filter. Water returns to the aquarium by overflowing through a waterfall-like chute. Outside power filters provide all three types of filtration. However, models containing some reusable media are more effective biological filters than models whose media must be completely replaced at each cleaning.

Undergravel filters sit beneath the gravel in your aquarium. They are powered by air pumps (which you place outside the tank) or powerheads (which fit on lift-tubes inside the tank). The filter draws water through the gravel and mechanically strains out solid particles. More important, helpful bacteria colonize the gravel bed and break down ammonia and other dissolved wastes. Undergravel filters are excellent biological and mechanical filters. Some brands use optional activated carbon cartridges to add minimal chemical filtration. Just remember, with undergravel filters your gravel is the filter media. If you don't use a gravel vacuum to clean the gravel regularly, the filter will clog and fail to function.

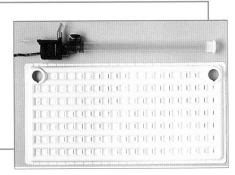

The undergravel filter plate sits on the bottom of your aquarium, under the layer of gravel.

Canister filters are the most versatile. They offer higher capacity, more choices in filtration media, and provide maximum water circulation. Canister filters are similar to a Shop Vac that sits below your aquarium and attaches to your aquarium with lengths of flexible tubing. Most canister filters provide all three types of filtration.

WARM AND HAPPY HEATERS

Most aquarium fish come from warm climates and require a temperature range of 75° to 78°F. An aquarium heater will prevent temperatures from falling below a set level. You can get a clamp-on heater that hangs on the back of the aquarium or a submersible model that is completely in the water, making it more childproof.

For tanks up to 50 gallons you'll need five watts of power per gallon, so a 20-gallon tank would need a 100-watt heater, for example. Over 50 gallons you'll need three watts per gallon, so a 55-gallon aquarium would need 165 watts, requiring a 200-watt heater (the closest size available).

Heaters get burning hot! Never place a hot heater into the water – the temperature difference can shatter the glass tube. And always unplug your heater and allow it to cool before removing it from the aquarium.

THERMOMETERS

Every aquarium needs a thermometer. How else will you know the water temperature? The most accurate, and easiest to read are liquid crystal thermometers that tape onto the outside of your

Thermometer

Gold marbled veiltail angelfish

tank. The old-fashioned glass thermometers that float around your tank are still available, as well. They are a bit less accurate, but you can use them to test the temperature of a bucket of water.

AIR PUMPS

Bubbles do not aerate your water; circulating water does. The exchange takes place at the water surface – carbon dioxide escapes and oxygen reabsorbs. So if you have a filter that circulates your water, there is probably no need for you to buy an air pump.

However, air pumps do have their uses. They can power an undergravel filter or they can power a box filter. They can power decorations, too. You can connect your air pump to a large airstone or bubble wall to make a cascade of decorative bubbles. You can also use an air pump to operate action ornaments, such as a treasure chest that opens and closes or a deep sea diver.

TUBING AND VALVES

Don't forget to pick up air line tubing to go with your air pump. The pump sits outside the aquarium and the tubing connects the air supply to the ornaments or filters inside the tank. If you want to run more than one item off a single pump, you may also need a gang-valve. A gang-valve divides your pump's output into two to five separate, controllable outlets. And remember, tee fittings are for combining two outlets into one, not splitting one into two.

Gold pearl angelfish

13

MORE TO BUY

I've talked about the main systems of your aquarium. Now you need a few more things to round out the setup.

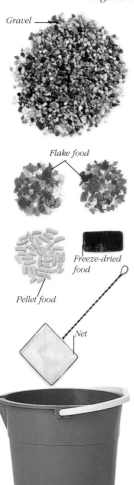

Gravel

Flake food

Freeze-dried food

Pellet food

Net

GRAVEL

Choose gravel with a pebble size of one-eighth to one-quarter inch. Smaller particles pack too tightly or filter through the slits in an undergravel filter. The spaces between larger particles enable food to become trapped out of reach of the fish, where it will pollute the tank. Buy enough gravel to make a layer 1.5 inch to 2 inches deep (usually that's about 1.5 pounds per gallon). Fish show their best colors when kept with dark-colored gravel.

FOOD

Variety is best. I suggest choosing a staple flake food, a freeze-dried food, and a live or frozen food.

FISH NET

Choose a size appropriate for the fish you will be catching. Green coarse nets are faster and more maneuverable in the water. White fine nets are slower and a bit more clumsy, but less likely to snag a fish's fins.

WATER CONDITIONER

You need to remove chlorine or chloramine from your tapwater to make it safe for your fish. The dealer in your aquarium supply store will know what's in the local tapwater and can help you pick a brand.

FISH-ONLY BUCKET

Soap kills fish. Buy a separate bucket for your aquarium maintenance chores, mark it "fish only" and make sure everyone knows not to use it for anything else.

GRAVEL VACUUM

Nothing makes your maintenance chores easier. Gravel vacuums clean your gravel while removing water for your regular partial water changes. You can even buy brands that hook to your sink to both drain and fill the aquarium.

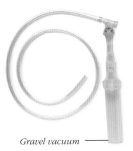

Gravel vacuum

ALGAE SCRUB PAD

Use it to keep the glass clean. Handheld pads reach into corners better than the kind that come mounted on a handle.

TEST KITS

You cannot tell the quality of your water by looking at it. You must test. Pick up pH, ammonia, and nitrite test kits.

BACKGROUND

An aquarium background sets off your aquarium and hides unsightly electrical cords, air lines, and filters that hang behind the tank. It attaches right to the back of your tank

DECORATIONS

Be artistic! I prefer natural rocks, driftwood, and live plants, but you can also use plastic plants, castles, divers, and so forth.

BOOK

This book is a basic primer. For a more detailed guide, check out the other titles in the More to Learn section on page 60.

Never use decorations that you've picked up from the beach or the park. They will slowly leech minerals into your tank that could harm your fish.

THE AQUATIC GREEN THUMB

Beautiful fish are the main attraction in an aquarium, but if you really want your aquarium to reflect the beauty of nature, you need to complement the fish with plants. Plants soften the harshness of a bare aquarium and provide cover for the fish. They act as spawning sites for egg-scattering species, and baby fish avoid being eaten by hiding out in the foliage.

BUNCH PLANTS

Anacharis
Hygrophila
Rotala indica
Water wisteria

CROWN PLANTS

Amazon swordplant
Anubias
Wisteria
Sagittaria
Vallisneria

FLOATING PLANTS

Hornwort

PLANTS TO AVOID
Some plants sold in aquarium stores are actually terrestrial or bog (semi-aquatic) species. They won't survive long underwater. Avoid the following plants:

- Princess pine
- Brazilian swordplant
- Mondo grass
- Aluminum plant

- Bella palm
- Purple crinkle
- Dragon's flame

Amazon sword plant

LIVE PLANTS

Live plants are dynamic. They grow and bend in the current. Your aquarium will look a little different each day. Live aquatic plants may also provide a bit of oxygen and remove some unneeded nutrients from the water, and their leaves may help supplement the diet of herbivorous fish. Remember that live plants require three to five watts of lighting per gallon of water, so choose your lighting system accordingly.

Water wisteria

Live aquatic plants are available in several forms. Bunch plants are groups of cuttings banded together. Each stem has a multitude of leaves. Remove the bands before planting. Plant the cuttings as a group or singly. Crown plants are single plants with all leaves radiating from a point at the plant's base. They are often sold in pots. Floating plants drift with the current. Most species dangle roots in the water to absorb nutrients.

PLASTIC PLANTS

I am not a fan of plastic plants. I like my aquarium to be natural and alive. Still, plastic plants are a good choice for some hobbyists. They don't die, and they won't ever need pruning or fertilization. Once a little algae grows on plastic plants, they can look fairly real. Plastic plants don't need light, so high-powered lighting systems are unnecessary and the standard full-hood will suffice.

Hygrophilia

Valisneria

SOME ASSEMBLY REQUIRED

Once you buy your equipment, you will need to assemble it. This task can be intimidating because you will have products from several manufacturers — and no unified set of instructions. The following steps will give you some guidance in setting up your new aquarium. Be sure to read the manufacturers' instructions carefully before assembly.

1. Install the aquarium. First, position your aquarium stand. Make sure it is level. It should be far enough from the wall to allow room for hang-on-the-back filters, filter hoses, and electrical cords. If you bought an aquarium background, attach it to the aquarium now. Clean the glass with plain water. Don't use soap! Center the aquarium on top of the stand.

Don't pile up rocks; they could fall.

2. Add gravel and heavy decorations. Pre-rinse your aquarium gravel and place it in the bottom of the aquarium. Slope it so that it is slightly higher in back. (That way, sediment will tend to collect at the front for easy removal with a siphon hose.) Carefully position heavy decorations. Remember, if you bought an undergravel filter, you must place it in the tank before adding the gravel!

3. Fill the aquarium. Place a saucer on top the gravel and pour the water into it so you don't disturb the gravel. Mix hot and cold water to achieve the desired 75° to 78°F (use your thermometer to check!). Fill to the bottom edge of the top frame on glass aquariums. For acrylic tanks, fill to one-half to one inch from the top. Add a dechlorinating water conditioner to make the tapwater safe for fish.

Make a depression in the gravel and add your plants. Cover up the roots with gravel.

4. Add plants and decorations. It is usually best to position taller plants and decorations toward the back.

5. Install your filter. Follow the manufacturer's instructions for assembly and filter media installation.

6. Install your heater. Follow the manufacturer's directions for installation and calibration. Don't forget to install your thermometer, too. Do not plug in the heater until after it is in the water!

7. Install your lighting system. If you bought a full-hood or a strip light and glass canopy combination, you may need to cut out spaces in the rear plastic strip to allow space for hang-on-the-tank filters and heaters. Then, position the lighting system on top the tank.

8. Wait 24 hours before buying fish! Be patient.

You must be sure the tank is not leaking, the temperature is stable, and all the equipment works properly before you buy the fish.

Kennyi cichlid

WHAT'S IN YOUR WATER?

Local tapwater varies widely from region to region. The mineral content of local soils and rock strata influence the chemical make-up of groundwater. Even water drawn from two nearby wells may be quite different. Municipal water treatment plants further affect the water as it is processed into tapwater.

Gold marble angelfish

Most tapwater is not safe for fish without first being treated. Municipalities add chemicals – chlorine and chloramine are most common – to kill germs that are harmful to humans. Unfortunately, these chemicals will damage your fishes' gills and must be removed from the tapwater.

CHLORINE
Chlorine can be easily, and instantly, removed from your tapwater by any dechlorinating water conditioner. The typical dosage is one drop per gallon, or one teaspoon per ten gallons, depending on the brand. Simply follow the manufacturer's instructions.

CHLORAMINE
In some areas, the local water supply has high levels of dissolved organic matter. Chlorine added to the water can combine with this organic matter to form carcinogenic substances. So some municipalities add both chlorine and ammonia to the water. The two combine to create new compounds called chloramines, which don't combine with the organic matter in the water. A good water dechlorinator will also neutralize chloramines. The problem is that you then release the ammonia into the water. If you have a well-established tank, your

Brilliant rasbora

Glass catfish

biological filtration will quickly neutralize the ammonia and it won;t be a big deal. But in a new tank the ammonia can build up to deadly levels. The manager at your local fish store should know if your tapwater contains chloramines. If it does, consider adding some zeolite ammo-chips to remove the ammonia, or talk to the manager about what he or she uses to keep the water safe for the fish in the store.

pH

You may need to adjust the pH of your tapwater to make it safe for fish. pH is a measurement of acidity or alkalinity. It's measured on a scale from 0 to 7, with the lower numbers being more acid and the higher numbers being more alkaline. A pH ranging from 6.8 to 7.4 is generally safe, with a pH of 7 being suitable for the broadest range of species.

If your tapwater falls outside this range, you can add chemicals to adjust it. Sodium bicarbonate (baking soda) raises pH. Sodium biphosphate lowers it. Aquarium shops stock these and other chemicals for altering pH, as well as pH kits for testing the water. I'll explain more about adjusting the pH of the water in your tank on page 52.

It's a good idea to test the pH of your tapwater, but you won't get an accurate reading if you test it straight from the tap. That's because tapwater has been stored under pressure in your local water system, and will have gasses dissolved in it. And some gasses affect pH. To get an accurate reading of your water's pH, put it in a jar and shake it for a few minutes before testing. This will drive out any excess gasses and allow the regular gasses that are in the air all around us to be absorbed, so you'll get a more accurate reading. There's no need to aerate water you're testing from the tank, though – your filter has already aerated it for you.

HOW MANY FISH?

Don't overcrowd your aquarium! This is one of the most common mistakes made by new hobbyists. Your local aquarium shop may offer hundreds of tempting varieties of exotic fish. With all those choices, it's easy to find a reason to want to add more fish to your tank. But overcrowding kills fish. The primary way that it kills is with pollution. The amount of waste in your aquarium is directly proportional to the number and size of the fish. More fish equals more waste. Your fish live in this waste. Filter systems and regular partial water changes help control waste build-up and enable us to crowd more fish into the small space of an aquarium. Still, there are limits!

Pink ghost angelfish

Overcrowding kills in other ways, too. When you pack fish tighter together, there is more opportunity for territorial disputes. Fights ensue and death may result. Overcrowding also stunts growth. Your fish won't reach full size and will be less likely to breed. The stress of overcrowding encourages disease, too, and diseases spread much more quickly in a crowded aquarium.

THE BASIC RULE

Keep no more than one inch of fish per gallon of water. This popular rule works well for typical sizes of tropical fish — that is, fish that are two to three inches in standard length. (Standard length is measured from the tip of the nose to the end of the body, not counting the tail.)

THE EXCEPTIONS

The one-inch-per-gallon rule does not work for cycling a new tank (see page 28). The one-inch-per-gallon rule also does not work for large fish. As a fish grows, it not only increases in length, it also increases in height and breadth. If you can visualize ten one-inch baby oscars lined up in front of one ten-inch adult, you will see what I mean. Indeed, the adult has a mass approximately 1,000 times bigger than that of the little guys. When the fish are larger, keep fewer inches of fish per gallon.

The black neon tetra above is about one inch long, while the red oscar below grows to about ten inches. Ten tetras equals one oscar in length, but one oscar equals 1,000 tetras in mass.

FISH MASS CONVERSIONS

FISH LENGTH	EQUIVALENT IN ONE-INCH FISH	HOW MANY GALLONS OF WATER PER FISH THIS SIZE?
1 inch	1	1
2 inches	8	1
4 inches	64	2
6 inches	216	8*
12 inches	1,728	25*
24 inches	13,824	125*

*These figures assume regular weekly partial water changes to prevent waste build-up!

CONSIDERATIONS FOR MIXING FISH

You would think picking your first fish would be the easiest thing in the world. It's not. You must consider more than their beauty alone.

• **Swimming zone:** Choose a good mix of surface, midwater, and bottom dwellers to balance the appearance of your aquarium.

• **Sleeping habits:** Nocturnal fish hide all day and come out at night. Don't pick too many or you won't get to see them much.

• **Schooling behavior:** Keep a minimum of three of each schooling species you choose. Six or more of a kind is even better.

• **Diet:** Always be sure you know what a fish eats before you buy it. Some fish require live foods, for example. If you don't provide the right diet, the fish will starve.

• **Compatibility:** Fish fight over many things, including food and mates, but territorial fights are the most common. Allow enough room for territorial species to stake their individual claims.

GENERAL SPECIES RULES

Here are some pointers for common types of aquarium fish.

• **Algae-eaters:** Plecostomus and otocinclus are the best choices. The latter stay small and are active during the day.

• **Angelfish:** These fish don't mix with fin-nippers. The long fins are an easy target. Angels and other cichlids are territorial.

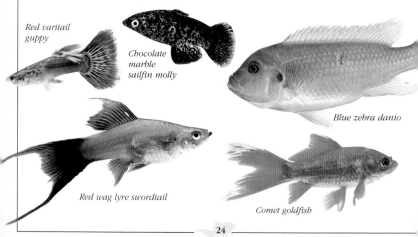

Red varitail
guppy

Chocolate
marble
sailfin molly

Blue zebra danio

Red wag lyre swordtail

Comet goldfish

- **Barbs:** Generally peaceful, but occasionally nippy. Barbs are best kept in small groups, especially tiger barbs.
- **Bettas (Siamese fighting fish):** Highly territorial. No more than one betta per tank. Don't mix the long-finned males with fin-nipping species.
- **Catfish:** Most are nocturnal. Some are predatory. The various corydoras cats are peaceful scavengers and are active during the day.
- **Danios:** Highly active and best kept in groups.
- **Goldfish:** Best kept separately from tropical fish, as they prefer cooler water and grow quite large.
- **Gouramies:** Keep only a single fish or pair of each species to avoid fighting. Be aware that some color varieties constitute a single species.
- **Guppies:** Peaceful livebearers. Fancy guppies are more delicate than the common guppy.
- **Mollies:** These livebearers do best with addition of one or two teaspoons of aquarium salt per gallon. They like extra algae or vegetation in the diet.
- **Platies (Moons):** These peaceful livebearers are available in many colors. Keep two females for each male.
- **Sharks:** Rainbow and red-tail sharks are territorial. Keep only one. Bala and iridescent sharks like to school, but get large.
- **Swordtails:** Colorful, peaceful livebearers. Keep two females for each male.
- **Tetras:** Generally peaceful. Tetras are best kept in schools.

Red-tailed
black shark

Glowlight tetra

Black marbled veiltail
angelfish

Filament barb

Red wag high-fin platy

Suckermouth
catfish

MODEL COMMUNITIES

Here are some sample communities of fish that will mix well. Notice that each group is listed in two batches. The first batch consists of a few hardy fish for cycling the new tank. After the aquarium has cycled, you may add the second batch. Feel free to substitute fish of similar size and behavior for the species on this list.

10-GALLON COMMUNITY

BATCH 1	BATCH 2
3 zebra or pearl danios	3 platies
2 corydoras catfish	3 neon tetras
	1 otocinclus

Neon tetra

Zebra danio

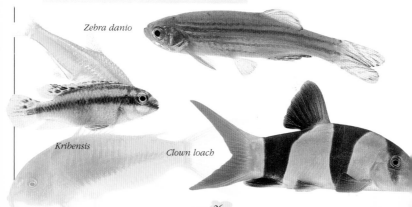

Kribensis

Clown loach

29-GALLON COMMUNITY

BATCH 1	BATCH 2
1 pair dwarf gouramies	6 neon tetras
3 platies	6 harlequin rasboras
6 black tetras	3 otocinclus or
3 corydoras catfish	1 small plecostomus

Sunset marigold high-fin platy

Dwarf gourami

Sunset platy

55-GALLON COMMUNITY

BATCH 1	BATCH 2
6 zebra or pearl danios	2 kissing gouramies
6 platies	1 pair kribensis
6 tiger barbs	3 clown loaches
12 serpae tetras	12 large neon tetras
	6 corydoras catfish
	6 otocinclus

Green tiger barb

Bronze corydoras catfish

ALL ABOUT THE NITROGEN CYCLE

You can help establish good bacteria in your tank by adding a handful of gravel from an established tank. Ask at your aquarium store.

Fish excrete ammonia. Established aquariums contain helpful bacteria that break down the ammonia, but new aquariums do not. You must cycle a new aquarium or your fish will poison themselves with their own ammonia.

WHAT HAPPENS DURING THE NITROGEN CYCLE?
Once you add fish to your aquarium, they will begin excreting ammonia and other wastes into the water. Ammonia levels will start to climb. Helpful bacteria will develop to break down this ammonia, but they take a week or more to develop, and the interim is a dangerous time. Once these helpful bacteria establish themselves, ammonia levels will drop back to zero.

However, the danger won't be over because the helpful bacteria convert the ammonia to nitrite – which is also toxic to fish. So as ammonia levels drop, nitrite levels will climb. A second group of helpful bacteria will establish itself and convert the nitrite to relatively harmless nitrate. This process will take another week or more.

The nitrate end-product will be kept under control by your regular partial water changes. Do not neglect to make these changes!

This entire process (ammonia to nitrite to nitrate) is known as the nitrogen cycle. That's why we refer to the process as cycling the aquarium. Cycling your aquarium usually takes two to three weeks, but it may take a month or more. Each aquarium is different.

SAFE CYCLING

1. First, start with a light load of fish. Your first batch should contain no more than half an inch of fish per gallon of water. In other words, no more than five inches of fish in a ten-gallon aquarium. After the tank cycles, you can add more fish to bring the total up to one inch of fish per gallon.

2. Be patient! Do not buy additional fish until both ammonia and nitrite levels have peaked and then subsided to undetectable levels. This will happen anywhere from two to six weeks after adding your first batch of fish. Remember, the clock doesn't start ticking until you add the first small batch of fish, because the fish produce the ammonia that gets the process started.

3. Buy an ammonia test kit and a nitrite test kit and use them. The only way to be sure your tank has cycled (and that it is safe to add the rest of your fish) is to run water tests. You cannot tell by looking at the aquarium.

The harmful chemicals that build up in your tank are invisible, and you may not see their effects on your fish until it is too late. Test the water daily with your ammonia and nitrite test kits so you know for sure that your aquarium has safely cycled.

THE HOMECOMING

Your fishes' first day home is a risky one. It is up to you to safely transport the fish home and to carefully introduce them to your aquarium.

TRANSPORTATION

When you buy fish for your aquarium, the personnel at the store will package them in plastic bags for the trip home. Each fish bag will contain two-thirds water and one-third air. The top of the bag is either knotted or bound with a rubber band. It will then be put inside a paper grocery sack.

Handle the bags carefully, so that you do not puncture them. Protect the fish from temperature extremes on the way home. Try to make the aquarium store your last stop for the day, so the fish don't spend too much time waiting for you to take them home. Keep the outer paper sack closed to help keep the temperature stable. Do not leave the fish unattended in the car. A fish can quickly freeze in the winter or cook on a hot summer day, even if the temperature seems fine to you. Also, do not position the fish bag too close to the heating and cooling ducts of your car.

WATCH THOSE SPIKES

Your aquarium dealer should double-bag spiny species, such as catfish and cichlids, to prevent punctures. Have him or her place the first bag upside-down in the second bag. Then, when the bag is sealed, all corners will round off, eliminating places for a fish to lodge and poke through.

ACCLIMATION

When you arrive home, carefully remove the plastic fish bags from the sack. Turn off the light on your aquarium to help calm the fish, and float the unopened fish bags on top the water in your tank. Let the bags float for about 20 minutes. This will equalize the temperature in the bags to the temperature of the water in the aquarium, preventing temperature shock to the fish when you release them.

Then open each fish bag and gently net out the fish. Release it into its new home and discard the water in the bag. This will the reduce your chances of introducing disease from another tank into your aquarium. You may turn the light back on after a few minutes.

Net out each fish as gently as you can, and hold the bag closed on top while you put the fish into the tank. You don't want water from the bag spilling out into your aquarium.

COMMERCIAL FISH FOOD

Pineapple swordtail

Feeding a wide variety of foods is the best way to provide a balanced diet for your fish. Commercially prepared fish foods make it easy to provide variety.

Before you buy food for your fish, be sure that you understand their dietary requirements. Carnivores will want more meaty foods, while herbivores will need more plant matter in their diet. Don't forget to consider feeding behavior, as well. Floating food pellets are useless to bottom feeders, for example.

Flakes

FLAKE FOODS

Staple flakes are a popular starter, but don't neglect the other flake varieties. Color flakes, brine shrimp flakes, and spirulina algae flakes contain natural color enhancers. Flakes provide a convenient foundation for a balanced diet, but they are not enough by themselves.

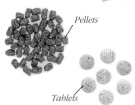

Pellets

Tablets

FOOD TABLETS AND PELLETS

Food tablets deliver nutrition to bottom feeders, while pellets are available in both sinking and floating forms. Floating pellets are for surface feeders.

Freeze-dried food

FREEZE-DRIED FOODS

Unlike flakes and pellets, which are highly processed blends of ingredients, freeze-dried foods are whole, natural aquatic organisms. They offer the nutritional value of live foods, but in a convenient dried form. Fish relish them because they provide a tasty, natural meal. Common examples are freeze-dried brine shrimp, daphnia, tubifex worms, bloodworms, plankton, and krill.

Frozen food

FROZEN FOODS

Offer frozen foods to your fish religiously. The nutrition of these foods is closest to that of natural live foods. The feeding response of your fish will show you how much they appreciate this kind of food, too. The same foods available freeze-dried are also available frozen. Additionally, you can find formulas consisting of mixes of assorted ingredients. Frozen foods come in flat packs or cube packs. Break off chunks of the flat pack to offer your fish. The cubes are even easier. Merely pop them out of the plastic tray and into your tank.

VACATION FOODS

Special time-release foods are available for when you are away. The foods consist primarily of a plaster block that dissolves slowly when you place it into your aquarium. As it dissolves, embedded food is exposed. Vacation foods have limited value, though. Sitting on the bottom of the tank, they offer nothing to the surface dwellers in your tank. The food also doesn't really stay fresh once it's exposed to water. A time-release feeder, or a friend who comes in to feed your fish, are better options when you're on vacation.

Time-release food

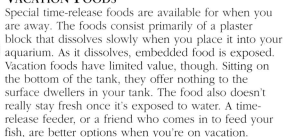
Red high-fin platy

Nissen's dwarf cichlid

LIVE FOODS

Nothing grabs the attention
of your fish like live foods.
They love wrestling with
the various worms, insects,
and crustaceans that you can
offer. The motion attracts them. The flavor
excites them. An exciting show results! Even
more important, live foods are nutritionally
complete. These natural aquatic creatures are exactly
the types of food your fish would feed on in the wild.

*Calico fantail
goldfish*

BRINE SHRIMP

Many dealers offer live adult brine shrimp for sale.
Live brine shrimp are great for conditioning
breeding stock. Your fish also love them as
treats. You can also buy cans of dry brine
shrimp eggs for hatching. Newly hatched brine
shrimp are a great first food for most baby
fish.

BLOODWORMS

These are not worms at all, but the aquatic
larvae of a harmless insect. The name comes
from the bright red color and long, worm-like
bodies. Bloodworms are more commonly offered
frozen and freeze-dried, but are now becoming available
live, as well.

FEEDER FISH

Big fish eat little fish. Feeder fish are prolific varieties sold in bulk –
usually several for a dollar. You can also buy them to keep as pets.
Cheap feeder fish are usually kept in crowded conditions, so be
careful not to introduce disease into your tank. The common guppy is
a small feeder fish; the rosy red minnow is a medium feeder fish, and
the common goldfish is a larger feeder fish.

GHOST SHRIMP

These interesting creatures are about an inch long and transparent as glass. You can actually see their stomachs change color to match the meal they just ate. In addition to being a food source for large fish, they can also be kept as scavengers with small fish.

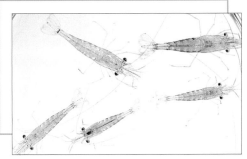

Ghost shrimp will be eaten by big fish, but can co-exist nicely with smaller fish.

MOSQUITO LARVAE

You can harvest your own mosquito larvae from ditches and standing containers of rainwater. Net them out, rinse them off, and feed them to your fish. Don't keep a large supply on hand, though, or you will soon have them transforming into pesky mosquitoes!

GLASSWORMS

These midge larvae look a bit like mosquito larvae, but are larger and completely

Rosy barb

transparent. Harvested from beneath the ice in winter, they are only available seasonally. All fish love them, but they may be too large for smaller fish.

BLACKWORMS

These tiny freshwater worms are one to two inches long and the diameter of a pencil lead. All fish love them, but bottom feeders especially relish them. Store unused blackworms in the refrigerator.

FEEDING CONSIDERATIONS

Feeding your fish gives you a chance to really interact with them.

You must avoid overfeeding your fish. Overfeeding results in uneaten food, which decays and pollutes your tank. And pollution will kill your fish.

A common rule says to think of a fish's stomach as being about the size of its eye. This will give you an idea of how much food a fish needs. In all cases, you should feed no more than will be consumed by all your fish in three minutes. If there is still food remaining in the tank after three minutes, you have overdone it and should siphon out the excess. Cut back at the next feeding.

WHEN TO FEED

Feed your fish twice a day. I suggest feeding once in the morning and once in the evening. Put one person in charge of feeding, so that the fish are not fed too frequently by accident.

Many species are nocturnal. If you feed the right amount during the day, there will be no food left for them when they come searching at night. The plecostomus is a good example. Most hobbyists buy them to eat algae, but if there is not enough algae you must supplement with other foods. Consider dropping an algae wafer into the tank when you turn off the lights.

HOW TO FEED

Never pour food directly from the container into your aquarium. There is too much chance that you will overdo it and pollute the tank. Always measure the food into your hand first. Then you'll be able to adjust any errors before adding the food to the aquarium.

• Flakes can be simply sprinkled onto the water surface (after first sprinkling them into your hand, of course).

• Sinking tablets should be targeted to reach the desired bottom feeding species.

• Most freeze-dried foods can be sprinkled onto the water surface. Freeze-dried tubifex worms come as cubes that can be pressed against the inside glass. They will stick there to be nibbled by the fish.

• Frozen foods can simply be tossed into the aquarium, although many hobbyists like to thaw them a bit first.

When you are the designated feeder, your fish will soon learn that their meals come from you. They may even start to recognize you, and come flocking to the front of the tank whenever you come near. As their feeder, it's your responsibility to make sure the top and bottom feeders both get fed, and that there's plenty for the fish that are active all day and the fish that are active at night.

EVERYDAY CARE

TURN ON THE LIGHT

The first thing you want to do in the morning is turn on the fish's light. Remember, though, that fish don't have eyelids. So it can be quite a shock to go from complete darkness to sudden brilliance. Turn on the room lights for a few minutes beforehand to allow time for their eyes to adjust. And remember to turn the light off before you go to bed.

CHECK THINGS OUT

Look at the aquarium to see if anything is out of whack. If there are any leaks, it will be very obvious. Look for the following, as well:

• Are there any dead fish? Look at the surface for floaters, look along the bottom for sinkers, check that there are no bodies wedged in the rocks or plants, and look midwater for any corpses that are drifting with the current. Dead fish should be rare (if they're not, you've got a problem), but it's always wise to check because decaying dead fish can pollute your tank and spread disease.

• Are any fish missing? Count them. Missing fish may be hiding, may have been eaten, or may have jumped out onto the floor!

• Check the water temperature. Is it within the proper range? Is the heater working?

• Are the fish behaving properly? Is anyone gasping at the surface or lying around abnormally? When you first turn on

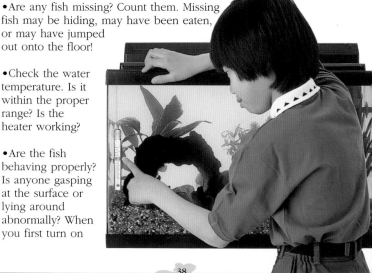

Cardinal tetra

the light, your fish may be a little sleepy. But if they're still lethargic a few minutes later, take a closer look.

- Are there any signs of disease on the fish, such as dots, slime, or fuzz?

- Are the filters working properly? Are the bubblers bubbling? These devices are the life support systems of your aquarium, so you need to give them a quick check every day.

All of this may sound like a lot of work, but it will take only a few seconds. Besides, you are going to be looking at your aquarium every day anyway, right?

FEEDING

Your primary daily duties will be offering your fish their two daily feedings. This should take just a minute or two. It is fun to watch the fish eat, but also take the opportunity to watch for any fish that is not eating. It may help you spot a disease problem early on. And don't forget to close the lid on the tank when you finish feeding, or the fish might jump out.

OTHER DUTIES

If you are cycling a new tank, be sure to run your ammonia and nitrite tests every day. When you have finished cycling your tank, you can do water tests once a week. Once you are satisfied that your water quality is stable, you can test it every other week.

Dwarf chained loach

Emperor tetra

TAKING CARE OF THE EQUIPMENT

If the equipment doesn't work properly in your tank, your fish will die.

The largest part of your aquarium investment will be in equipment, but if you take care of it most equipment will last a lifetime. Even better, required maintenance will be minimal.

OUTSIDE POWER FILTER

There are too many brands of filters and styles of filter media to list here. Follow your manufacturer's instructions. Outside power filters use disposable filter media. Replace this media monthly. If the filter clogs before that, you can either replace it sooner or try rinsing the media to get the full month from it. If your filter uses sponge filter blocks, those can be rinsed and reused forever. Replace activated carbon monthly, regardless of how clean it looks, because there is no way to tell when the carbon is saturated. Occasionally remove your filter's impeller and clean the impeller well with a brush or cotton swab.

UNDERGRAVEL FILTER

Your gravel is the filter media for your undergravel filter. Use a gravel vacuum to siphon out detritus at every regular partial water change (see pages 43 and 48 for more on using the gravel vacuum).

CANISTER FILTER

Most canister filters use more than one style of filter medium. As always, replace activated carbon or other chemical filter media monthly. Sponges, ceramic noodles, and crushed lava rock can be rinsed and reused indefinitely. Pleated cartridges and some other types of polyester media bear some rinsing and reuse, but will eventually become clogged and need to be replaced. Buy the media recommended by the filter's manufacturer and follow the manufacturer's instructions.

AIR PUMP

If your model has an air filter pad on the bottom, replace it as needed – usually once or twice a year. Clear clogged gang-valves with a paperclip. Clogged airstones produce back-pressure that eventually cracks the diaphragm of your pump. Change airstones every three to six months to extend the life of your pump. Aquarium stores sell replacement diaphragms, if you need one.

LIGHTS

Although fluorescent bulbs may burn for three years, they lose intensity as they age. It is best to replace them each year. Also replace the starter cylinder when you change the bulb. Replace incandescent bulbs when they burn out.

HEATER

Check regularly to be sure no water has entered the heater.

Dissolved minerals in the water can build up on all your equipment as water sloshes and splashes. Regular cleaning of all surfaces will prevent this build-up.

KEEPING THE TANK CLEAN

A magnetic scraper will clean the inside of the tank while you keep dry.

CLEAN THE GLASS

Plain water and a paper towel work best for cleaning the outside glass. It is okay to use window cleaning solutions on the outside glass only. Window cleaning solutions are deadly to fish, so be very careful to get none inside the aquarium.

Aquarium stores stock an assortment of scrapers and scrub pads for removing algae from the inside glass, but simple handheld algae scrub pads work best. Yes, you will have to get your hands wet to use them, but they are more maneuverable, working easily into tight corners. You can also find scrapers and scrubbers with long handles for occasional touch-ups. Magnet scrapers come in two pieces – the scraping half goes inside the tank and a magnetic handle goes on the outside. When you move the outer magnetic handle, it pulls the scraper along the inner glass.

Use only soft scrubber pads on acrylic aquariums to prevent scratching. Never use household cleaning sponges in your aquarium. They are impregnated with toxic chemicals!

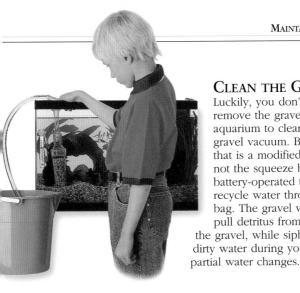

CLEAN THE GRAVEL

Luckily, you don't have to remove the gravel from the aquarium to clean it. Use a gravel vacuum. Buy the kind that is a modified siphon hose, not the squeeze bulb or battery-operated types that recycle water through a mesh bag. The gravel vacuum will pull detritus from deep within the gravel, while siphoning out dirty water during your regular partial water changes.

CLEAN THE DECORATIONS

Decorations with smooth surfaces can usually be wiped off with an algae scrubber pad. If the surface of the decoration is too rough for that, you may soak it in a solution of half a cup of bleach per bucket of water. A ten- to thirty-minute soak should kill and loosen algae. Remember that bleach is lethal to fish. Always rinse decorations after bleaching, and soak them further in plain water to remove all traces of bleach before returning them to your tank. Also, bleach may discolor some decorations. Use it with great care.

OTHER CLEANING

Wipe off your full-hood, filters and heaters as needed. A damp rag will usually work. Scrub built-up mineral deposits with a toothbrush and a bit of vinegar. Do not get vinegar in your tank!

Make sure all your fish cleaning buckets, sponges, and brushes are used only for the fish. Any exposure to household chemicals can be deadly for your fish.

DEALING WITH AGGRESSION

You picked compatible species and didn't overcrowd. You made sure you knew the special dietary and housing requirements of your fish beforehand. Right? So everything should go smoothly. Still, even the best-laid plans can go awry.

Fish fight for many reasons. They fight to protect territory. They fight to protect mates or drive off rivals. And they fight to establish a pecking order. Most fights are harmless. It is part of daily life, and life goes on. However, if damage occurs, you may need to take action.

WARNING SIGNS

Fights are usually obvious. If you see two fish beating the scales off each other, you know you have a problem. But you may not always witness the fight. So look for these warning signs:

• **Torn fins:** Tattered fins are usually the result of aggression. Split fins are minor and should heal quickly without attention. If chunks of fin are missing, action may be needed.

• **Sores:** Small red marks may heal unaided. Bloody patches require medication.

• **Locked jaws:** Many species wrestle with their mouths. If torn lips and scratched faces result, the fights are probably serious. Mock battles constitute breeding behavior in some species, though. And the interesting kissing gouramies kiss each other to mark territorial boundaries.

Sometimes aggression is not so obvious. Get to know your fish. Learn what is normal behavior for each species and individual. The following symptoms may indicate aggression is occurring out of sight:

• **Loss of appetite:** When one fish bullies another away from food, the victim may give up eating entirely.

• **Hiding:** Bullied fish seek shelter. These fish usually display physical damage, as well.

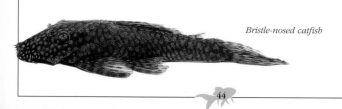
Bristle-nosed catfish

Move the bully to an isolation tank, rather than the victim. If you remove the victim, the aggressor may just pick on another victim.

TAKING ACTION

If you see a fight, you might want to break it up. Give your fish a chance to work out their territorial boundaries if you can, but if things are getting serious a few taps on the glass or the sudden appearance of the fish net in the tank may be all that's needed to distract the combatants.

If your fish show damage or signs of being bullied, you may need to take action. Consider the following:
• Separate the aggressor in another aquarium, or place it in a net breeder basket to isolate it.
• If the victim's wounds are minor, allow it to heal in the aquarium. Other fish tend to pick at wounds, though, so separation into a net breeder basket may be necessary for peaceful healing.
• Place severely damaged individuals into an isolation tank for medication, to prevent infection from setting in.

ADDING TO THE COMMUNITY

Be patient and wait until your tank has completely cycled before you add more fish.

ADDING FISH TO A NEWLY CYCLED TANK

Remember that you should introduce no more than one-half inch of fish for each gallon of water while you're cycling your new tank. After the tank has cycled, you may add more fish to bring your total to one inch of fish per gallon.

ADDING FISH TO AN ESTABLISHED AQUARIUM

Properly cared for, your fish should live for years. Still, a time may come when you need to replace one, or just feel like adding a new fish to an existing tank. As I've already described on page 30, be sure to protect new arrivals from temperature shock on the way home. Float new fish bags on top of your aquarium for 20 minutes to allow the temperature of the water inside the bag to synchronize with the temperature of your aquarium.

A new arrival is at a disadvantage. Existing inhabitants have staked out all the territories in your aquarium and may attack new arrivals. Before adding a new fish to an inhabited aquarium, take these precautions:

New arrivals will be the target of much curiosity, but may also be the target of aggression.

• Feed the fish that are already in the tank. If their stomachs are full, they will be less likely to take nips at the new arrivals.
• If you keep aggressive or highly territorial fish, it may be wise to rearrange the decorations before adding new fish. This forces existing residents to scramble for territory, just like the new arrivals. It takes away the home turf advantage and puts everyone on the same footing.
• Add a new decoration. A new rock or bunch of plants provides additional hiding places

QUARANTINE

You may want to set up a small isolation tank to quarantine new arrivals before introducing them to your established aquarium. A two-week quarantine will prevent the introduction of disease into your aquarium.

PARTIAL WATER CHANGES

Change 25 percent of your aquarium water every two weeks. This is probably the most important thing you can do for your fish. Your fish live in their own waste. Filters remove a certain amount of waste, but the rest remains dissolved in the aquarium water. Additionally, biological processes remove certain necessary minerals from the water. Partial water changes remove dissolved wastes and replace trace elements.

GRAVEL VACUUMS

A gravel vacuum is a simple siphon hose with a large tube at one end. You use the siphon hose to remove water for your regular partial water changes. The large tube vacuums detritus from the bottom as it siphons.

To start your gravel vacuum, place the entire device underwater in your aquarium. Let all the air bubble out of the hose, and then place your thumb over the small end of the hose. Keeping the large end under water, lift the small end of the hose from the aquarium, drop it down into a bucket on the floor, and release your thumb. Water will flow into the bucket.

While water flows into the bucket, poke the large end of the gravel vacuum into the gravel bed for a moment, and then lift it out of the gravel. The flow of water will be strong enough to rinse all debris from the gravel and into the bucket. However, the flow is not strong enough to remove the gravel, which is heavier and will drop back to the bottom. Continue poking the large tube into the gravel to clean more gravel. With a little practice, you will be able to clean the entire bottom while removing 25 percent of the water for your partial water change.

Dump the buckets of dirty water. Then rinse your bucket and use it to refill the tank with fresh, dechlorinated tapwater that's the same temperature as the water in your aquarium.

CLEAN AND FILL DEVICES

A variation of the gravel vacuum attaches to the faucet of your sink with a long hose. Water pressure from the sink powers the device, commonly called a python after one famous brand. The device vacuums waste and old water from the tank and flushes it into the drain of your sink. Afterward, you turn a switch and use the same hose to refill the aquarium. There is no need to carry a bucket.

By using a gravel vacuum to do your partial water changes, you are cleaning the bottom of the tank at the same time as you renew and refresh the water.

When you refill the tank, pour the water onto a saucer so the incoming stream does not disturb the fish, the gravel, or the plants.

pH AND OTHER WATER TESTS

While most fish like a neutral pH, some species, such as cichlids, like a little more alkalinity. Ask when you buy your fish.

Good water quality is most important to your fish. Despite what many people think, there is no way to tell how good your aquarium water is by looking at it. Just because the water is clear does not mean it is healthy for your fish. The only way to judge the quality of your water is to run tests. You really should keep the three test kits described here on hand, and use them regularly.

pH TEST
We measure pH on a scale of 0 to 14. A pH of 7 is neutral and is suitable for the broadest range of fish. A pH below 7 is acid, and a pH higher than 7 is alkaline (also called basic). The lower the pH, the more acidic the water is. The higher the pH, the more alkaline the water. Most fish fare well with a pH between 6.8 and 7.4. As your tank ages and waste builds up, pH tends to fall. Regular partial water changes will help maintain it at acceptable levels.

AMMONIA TEST
This test is especially important for the first week after adding fish. Fish produce ammonia as waste. In an established aquarium, there are helpful bacteria that neutralize the ammonia. Until these bacteria become established, ammonia levels can temporarily climb to lethal levels. The only acceptable ammonia level is zero. Ammonia is more toxic in alkaline water than in acidic water.

NITRITE TEST

This test is also important for the new aquarium. Helpful bacteria convert toxic ammonia into less toxic nitrite. Another group of bacteria will also develop to neutralize the nitrite by converting it to harmless nitrate. Strive for undetectable nitrite levels.

OPTIONAL TESTS

Local tapwater varies by region and may require additional testing. Ask the dealer at your aquarium store for further advice.

• **Nitrate** is not toxic, except in very high levels. High nitrate levels usually reflect overcrowding or insufficient water changes. Groundwater in farming areas may also be high in nitrates, as a result of the run-off of fertilizers.

• **General hardness** (GH) test kits measure water hardness. Dissolved calcium and magnesium are the largest contributors to water hardness.

• **Carbonate hardness** (KH) test kits measure substances that affect buffering capacity. Buffers are substances that help your water resist changes in pH.

Test your water daily when you are cycling your tank, and every other week after your aquarium is established and the water quality is stable.

TROUBLESHOOTING

ADJUSTING pH

You may need to adjust the pH of
your tapwater to make it safe for fish.
Your aquarium store sells products to do
so. Most common are concoctions of sodium
bicarbonate (baking soda) to raise pH, and sodium
biphosphate to lower pH. Each one-point change in pH represents a
tenfold change in acidity or alkalinity, so always adjust pH slowly –
no more than one full pH point per day.

Brown discus fish

The necessary amount of chemicals will vary greatly, depending on
the mineral content of your local tapwater. Always start with less
chemical than you think you need, and then add more to adjust. If
your water has a high general hardness (GH) or carbonate hardness
(KH), you may have a difficult time adjusting pH.

Remember that a pH of 6.8 to 7.4 is safe for most fish.
Adjustment within this range is generally unnecessary. Also,
the build-up of fish wastes causes pH to fall over time. Use
partial water changes, not chemicals, to adjust for that
decline.

*It's best not to adjust your pH, trying to
make it "perfect." If it's within the safe
range, it's easier on the fish to just adapt.*

Comet goldfish

DEALING WITH AMMONIA

You should normally only encounter detectable ammonia levels in a new, uncycled aquarium. The best thing to do for high ammonia levels in a new aquarium is usually nothing. If the fish look okay and none are dying, let the helpful bacteria develop that will fix the problem naturally. If the fish are showing signs of stress or are dying, consider the following:

• Do a partial water change to dilute the ammonia.

• Add zeolite (ammo-chips) to your filter.

• Add a product containing dormant bacteria, available from most aquarium stores.

Detectable ammonia levels in an established aquarium are signs of serious overcrowding, overfeeding, or destruction of biological filtration. Improve your fishkeeping practices!

HANDLING NITRITE

(We are talking about nitrite, not nitrate.) Like ammonia, nitrite should only be detectable in a new, uncycled aquarium in the later stages of the nitrogen cycle. If the levels are high but the fish look fine, simply wait for the helpful bacteria to develop that will fix the problem. If nitrite levels are high and your fish show obvious stress, consider the following steps:

• Do a partial water change to dilute the nitrite.

• Add one teaspoon of aquarium salt per gallon of water. It won't remove the nitrite, but it neutralizes the toxicity of it. This low level of salt will not hurt any species of fish.

SICKNESS AND HEALTH

SIGNS OF HEALTH

• A healthy fish tends to keep its fins fully splayed. Fins should not be torn.

• Eyes should be clear and undamaged.

• Good body weight is a requirement. Avoid emaciated fish.

• Bright, clean colors reflect health. There should be no patchiness to the complexion.

• Look for fish that are active and interested in life. (But remember that sedentary behavior is normal for some species, such as plecostomus.)

Flame tetra

SIGNS OF ILLNESS

• Bloody or slimy patches on the body or fins indicate infection.

• Clamped fins indicate a fish under stress. (But remember that clamped fins are normal on some species, such as plecostomus.)

• Ragged fins result from bites or infection. A grayish edge on torn fins indicates infection.

• Cloudy eyes may indicate disease or poor water quality.

• It is a bad sign when a normally active fish becomes reclusive.

• Emaciated and overly swollen stomachs are both warning signs.

• White, salt-sized dots on the skin indicate an ich infection.

• Rapid breathing may indicate parasites in the gills or poor water quality.

Fancy goldfish

FISH FIRST AID

The most common fish diseases are protozoal, bacterial, or fungal. Fish can also get viral infections, but they are untreatable.

Comet goldfish

• Ich: This protozoan forms small, salt-grain-sized white dots on the body or fins.

• Fin rot: Tattered and decayed areas on the edge of fins are signs of fin rot. In some cases the fin rays remain, but the interlacing fin structure rots away. Fin rot is usually bacterial, but may also be caused by protozoans.

• Mouth rot: Bacterial infections usually cause this problem, which manifests itself as a slime or cotton-like coating of the lips. Secondary protozoal infections may require additional treatment.

• Body rot: Open sores, bloody patches, and odd discoloration denote infections of the body tissues. In most cases bacterial infections are to blame, but advanced protozoal infections may cause the same symptoms.

• Fungus: The disease called mouth fungus or cottonmouth is often attributed to a fungus, but in fact it is caused by bacteria. True fungus attacks dead tissue. It forms a thick, fuzzy, hair-like patch on dead fish or decayed food – or establishes itself as an infection of dead tissue around open wounds of living fish.

Isolating a fish with a fungal infection in a quarantine tank will prevent other fish from nipping at the wounds and making them worse.

Six-barred distichodus

TREATING FISH DISEASES

Use an appropriate treatment for the type of infection you think your fish has. See your aquarium store dealer for recommended brands. And note that you must remove activated carbon from your filters during treatment.

• Protozoal infections: Treat ich and other protozoan infections with malachite green, or a combination of formalin and malachite green. In the case of ich, the medication will not kill the parasites on the fish. It is only effective when the parasites drop off to multiply. So treat the whole aquarium daily until the dots disappear from the fish, and then treat for an additional day or two to kill the free-swimming stage of the ich parasite.

• Bacterial infections: Use a good antibiotic. If only one fish has an infection, consider treating it in a quarantine tank. Treat for five days, but if there is no improvement after three, switch to a different antibiotic.

• True fungal infections: Preparations of sodium chlorite or methylene blue may be effective. Netting the fish and painting the wound with mercurochrome also helps.

ANTIBIOTICS FOR FISH

Ignore brand names; they are meaningless. Instead, look for active ingredients. Good results are obtained with the following:
• Sulfas: sulfamethazine, sulfamerazine, sulfathiozole, and others
• Furanoids: furazolidone, nitrofurazone, nifurpurinol, and others
• Kanamycin
• Minocycline

Avoid the following; they are relatively ineffective in aquariums:
• Penicillin
• Erythromycin
• Tetracycline (Terramycin)

YOUR FISH NEEDS YOU

Since fish don't have arms and legs, since they are not warm and fuzzy or warm and feathery, many people don't consider fish to be pets. How foolish! You will soon discover that your fish have their own charms and personalities.

It won't take your fish long to learn to recognize you. You will soon find them swarming to the front of the aquarium every time you are near. You will become their God or Goddess of the Fish Food Can who rains down manna from heaven upon them. Yes, your fish will always be happy to see you! You can even teach your fish to take food directly from your fingers. I used to have some oscars that would stick their faces completely out of the water to take food from my fingers.

Although you can't cuddle your fish in your arms like a puppy, many larger fish seem to enjoy being petted when they come up for food. Always pet lightly, though, so as not to wipe away the fish's protective slime coating.

Many hobbyists enjoy breeding their fish. When your fish have babies, you may feel like a proud grandparent. Raising up little ones is fun. Watching a pair of angelfish herding several hundred babies can be a special thrill.

And here's the best part: As you watch your aquarium, you will feel your tensions slipping away. Aquariums are relaxing to watch, and that is probably the greatest reward of all.

BEYOND DOLLARS AND CENTS

If you don't feed your fish or change their water, they will die. If you overcrowd your fish, mix incompatible species, or fail to maintain your equipment, the fish will not last long. If you are unwilling to do these things, you should not become a fishkeeper.

Although individual fish do not cost much, do not think of fish as cheap little expendables. The few pennies lost on the cost of the fish may not mean much to you, but don't forget that what you measured in money, the fish measured in suffering.

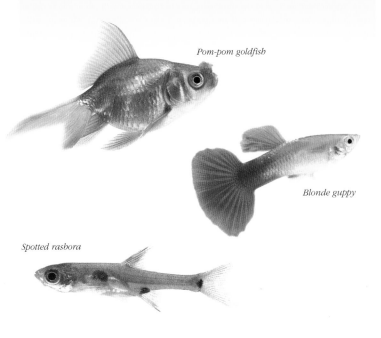

Pom-pom goldfish

Blonde guppy

Spotted rasbora

MORE TO LEARN

Platinum angelfish

BOOKS

Aquarium Atlas, Volumes 1-5, by Hans A. Baensch and
Dr. Rudiger Riehl, Microcosm

Dr. Axelrod's Atlas of Freshwater Aquarium Fishes, 9th Edition,
by Dr. Herbert Axelrod, et. al., T.F.H. Publications

KISS Guide to Freshwater Aquariums, by Mike Wickham,
Dorling Kindersley Publishing

KISS Guide to Saltwater Aquariums, by Mike Wickham,
Dorling Kindersley Publishing

The New Aquarium Handbook, Ines Scheurmann,
Barron's Educational Series

MAGAZINES

Aquarium Fish Magazine
Fancy Publications
PO Box 53351
Boulder, CO 80322
www.aquariumfish.com

Freshwater and Marine Aquarium
R/C Modeler Corp.
PO Box 487
Sierra Madre, CA 91025
www.mag-web.com/fama/

Practical Fishkeeping
Motorsport
550 Honey Locust Rd.
Jonesburg, MO 63351

Tropical Fish Hobbyist
T.F.H. Publications
One TFH Plaza
Neptune City, NJ 07753
www.tfh.com

AQUARIUM SOCIETIES

Contact these organizations for
the location of a club near you.

Federation of American Aquarium
Societies
4816 E. 64th St.
Indianapolis, IN 46220-4728
(317) 255-2523
www.tomgriffin.com/FAAS/

Ruby shark

Canadian Association of
Aquarium Clubs
298 Creighton Court
Waterloo, Ontario
Canada N2K 1W6
www.caoac.on.ca

PUBLIC AQUARIUMS
New York Aquarium
Boardwalk and West 8th St.
Brooklyn, NY 11224
www.nyaquarium.com

National Aquarium in Baltimore
Pier 3, 501 E. Pratt St.
Baltimore, MD 21202
www.aqua.org

John G. Shedd Aquarium
1200 S. Lake Shore Dr.
Chicago, IL 60605
www,sheddnet.org

Monterey Bay Aquarium
886 Cannery Row
Monterey, CA 93940
www.mbayaq.org

The Florida Aquarium
Harbour Island
Tampa, FL 33602
www.sptimes.com/Aquarium/

Aquarium of the Americas
Woldenberg Riverfront Park
New Orleans, LA 70130
www.audoboninstitute.org/html/
aa_aquarium.html

Waikiki Aquarium
2777 Kalakaua Ave
Honolulu, HI 96815
www.mic.hawaii.edu/aquarium

WEB SITES
Compuserve
go.compuserve.com/fishnet
(members use: GO FISHNET)

America Online
www.aol.com (members use
KEYWORD: PET CARE)

Aqualink
www.aqualink.com

Fish Information Service
www.actwin.com/fish/index.cgi

Fish Link Central
www.fishlinkcentral.com

The Krib
www.thekrib.com

ABOUT THE AUTHOR
Mike Wickham has been an aquarium hobbyist since 1964,
and an aquarium retailer for more than 20 years. He writes
for *Aquarium Fish* and *Aquarium USA* magazines, and is a
resident expert on Compuserve's Fish Forum and for
pets.com. Mike is also the author of two best-selling books
on aquarium set-up and care.

INDEX

Royal blus discus fish

Dorling  Kindersley

LONDON, NEW YORK, SYDNEY, DELHI, PARIS,
MUNICH, JOHANNESBURG

Project Editor: Beth Adelman
Design: Carol Wells
Cover Design: Gus Yoo
Photo Research: Mark Dennis, Martin Copeland, Romaine Werblow
Index: Nanette Cardon

Photo Credits: Paul Bricknell, Mike Dunning, Max Gibbs, Dave King, Jerry Young

First American Edition, 2000
2 4 6 8 10 9 7 5 3 1

Published in the United States by
Dorling Kindersley Publishing, Inc. 95 Madison Avenue New York, New York 10016

Dorling Kindersley Publishing, Inc. offers special discounts for bulk purchases for sales promotions
or premiums. Specific, large-quantity needs can be met with special editions, including
personalized covers, excerpts of existing guides, and corporate imprints. For more information,
contact Special Markets Department, Dorling Kindersley Publishing, Inc.,
95 Madison Avenue, New York, NY 10016 Fax: (800) 600-9098.

Color reproduction by Colourscan, Singapore
Printed in Hong Kong by Wing King Tong

Library of Congress Cataloging-in-Publication Data
Wickham, Mike.
    What your fish needs / Mike Wickham.-- 1st American ed.
        p. cm. -- (What your pet needs)
Includes index.
    ISBN 0-7894-6309-1 (alk. paper)
    1. Aquarium fishes. 2. Aquariums. I. Title. II. Series.
SF457 .W52 2000
639.34--dc21
00-008258

See our complete catalog at
www.dk.com